# How to use this book

*Follow the advice, in italics, where given.*
*Support the children as they read the text that is shaded in cream.*
**Praise** *the children at every step!*
*Detailed guidance is provided in the Read Write Inc. Phonics Handbook.*

**8 reading activities**
*Children:*
1  *Practise reading the speed sounds.*
2  *Read the green and red words for the non-fiction text.*
3  *Listen as you read the introduction.*
4  *Discuss the vocabulary check with you.*
5  *Read the non-fiction text.*
6  *Re-read the non-fiction text and discuss the 'questions to talk about'.*
7  *Re-read the non-fiction text with fluency and expression.*
8  *Practise reading the speed words.*

# Speed sounds

| f | l<br>ll | m | n | r | s | v | z<br>s | (sh) | (th) | ng<br>nk |
|---|---|---|---|---|---|---|---|---|---|---|

| b | c<br>k<br>(ck) | d | g | h | j | p | qu | t | w | x | y | ch<br>tch |
|---|---|---|---|---|---|---|---|---|---|---|---|---|

**Vowels** *Say the vowel sound and then the word, e.g. 'a', 'at'.*

| at | hen | in | on | up | day | see | high | blow | zoo |
|---|---|---|---|---|---|---|---|---|---|

*Each box contains one sound but sometimes more than one grapheme. Focus graphemes are **circled**.*

*Read in Fred Talk (pure sounds).*

| | | | | | |
|---|---|---|---|---|---|
| fast | tram | tru<u>ck</u> | six | <u>sh</u>ip | <u>th</u>is |
| sled | jet | bus | pu<u>ll</u> | | |

*Read in syllables.*

ro<u>ck</u>` et  ➞  ro<u>ck</u>et

*Read the root word first and then with the ending.*

dog  ➞  dogs    lot  ➞  lots

**Red words**

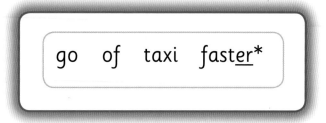

go   of   taxi   fast<u>er</u>*

*red for this book only

# Let's go!

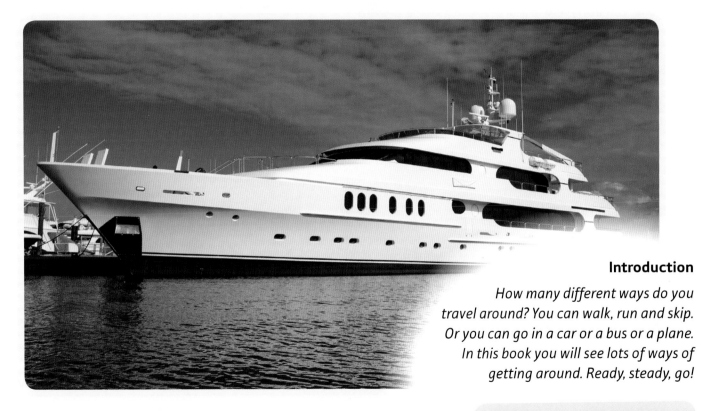

### Introduction

*How many different ways do you travel around? You can walk, run and skip. Or you can go in a car or a bus or a plane. In this book you will see lots of ways of getting around. Ready, steady, go!*

**Written by Gill Munton**

# Vocabulary check

*Discuss the meaning (as used in the non-fiction text) after the children have read the word.*

|  | definition |
|---|---|
| **taxi** | *a car with a driver who you pay to take you somewhere* |
| **tram** | *a bit like a bus, but it travels on a special track* |
| **sled** | *for travelling on snow and ice, pulled by dogs* |
| **jet** | *a very fast plane* |

**Punctuation to note:**

| Let's Six | *Capital letters that start sentences* |
|---|---|
| . | *Full stop at the end of each sentence* |
| ! | *Exclamation mark* |
| . . . | *'Wait and see' dots* |

Let's go ...

... in a van ...

... in a truck.

Let's go ...

... in a taxi ...

... in a tram.

Let's go ...

... on a big ship.

Let's go ...

... on a dog sled.
Six dogs pull this sled.

Let's go ...

... on a bus.

Lots of us can go on a bus!

13

Let's go fast!
Let's go ...

... up in a jet.

Let's go faster!
Let's go ...

... up in a rocket.

Let's go!

# Questions to talk about ⭐

**FIND IT**
- ✓ *Turn to the page*
- ✓ *Read the question*
- ✓ *Find the answer*

*Page 12:*     *How many dogs pull the sled?*

*Page 13:*     *What can lots of people travel on?*

*Pages 14–15:*  *What two things can we go up in?*

*Page 15:*     *What goes faster than a jet?*

# Speed words

*Children practise reading the words across the rows, down the columns and in and out of order clearly and quickly.*

| van | fast | ship | sled | go |
|-----|------|------|------|-----|
| can | up | this | tram | lots |
| jet | a | truck | dog | in |
| big | six | of | pull | bus |